Happy Birthday, the Cat

Happy Birthday, the Cat

TRUE MEOW STORIES BY BIRTHDAY
TRANSCRIPTIONS AND PHOTOGRAPHS BY NORIKO AND DON CARROLL

Andrews McMeel
Publishing

Kansas City

03 04 05 06 07 WKT 10 9 8 7 6 5 4 3 2 1

Library of Congress Cataloging-in-Publication Data

Carroll, Noriko.
   Happy Birthday, the cat : true meow stories / by Birthday ; transcriptions and photographs by Noriko and Don Carroll.
      p.cm.
   ISBN 0-7407-3317-6
      1. Cats—Fiction. 2. Cat owners—Fiction. 3. Human-animal relationships—Fiction.
   I. Carroll, Don, 1938– II. Title.

      PS3603.A7746 H37 2003
      813'.6—dc21

                                                    2002034272

Attention: Schools and Businesses

Andrews McMeel books are available at quantity discounts with bulk purchase for educational, business, or sales promotional use. For information, please write to: Special Sales Department, Andrews McMeel Publishing, 4520 Main Street, Kansas City, Missouri 64111.

For Sonja
and
everyone who ever had a birthday

Acknowledgments

My parents took pictures of me from the first day, and I'm glad. Growing up in a New York commercial photo studio, I was part of the action every day, and there was always a camera within reach. I was captured on film no matter what I was doing—eating, sleeping, playing, even doing my business! Mamma and Papa were like first-time parents who couldn't help but take pictures of their new baby, and they always showed my funny pictures to friends like Sonja Bullaty and Angelo Lomeo, who are famous photographers. Auntie Sonja had a cat allergy and couldn't touch me, but she loved me dearly and told me I should write a book. I visualized myself signing books with my paw. Both she and Uncle Angelo inspired us, and I am so grateful to them. Sadly, Auntie Sonja passed away in Fall 2000, so I persuaded my parents to work with me on the book.

We edited three thousand pictures of me. Mama and Papa complained that my fur kept falling on the slides after I edited them. I told Mama a story, and she listened quietly, then processed the tale through her Japanese sensibility. While she was working, I told Papa another story. He constantly interrupted with outrageous comments and made me roll on the floor laughing. It was hard to get any work done that way, so Mama designed the whole book by herself.

Uncle Punk (Alberto Rizzo) was with us from the first day, and his sense of humor and great artistry had a strong influence on everyone. Tony and Angel of Little Italy, who rescued me from the cold streets of New York; Topi and Cao Yong; Jay Reiburn, aka Dr. J; the four turtles; Dr. Duck; Mikky the mouse; Luci and her family; Larry and Caroline Amoruso; Jay Maisel; Nancy Parinello; Nance, Nick, and Sophie Abadilla; Jay and Joy Donohue; and many more friends encouraged and supported us as we created this book. I meowfully thank them all.

I especially want to thank Al Zuckerman of Writer's House in New York, who instantly recognized my literary genius as the new cat on the block, and Chris Schillig, our insightful editor at Andrews McMeel who shaped up our exotic, dyslexic cat grammar and expressions. Last but not least, many thanks to my grandparents, Tokuko and Shinichi Iizuka; Uncle Nobuyoshi; and Aunt Yumiko for their love and continuous support for us. I hope you can feel the joy of meow life in my book.

Happy Birthday

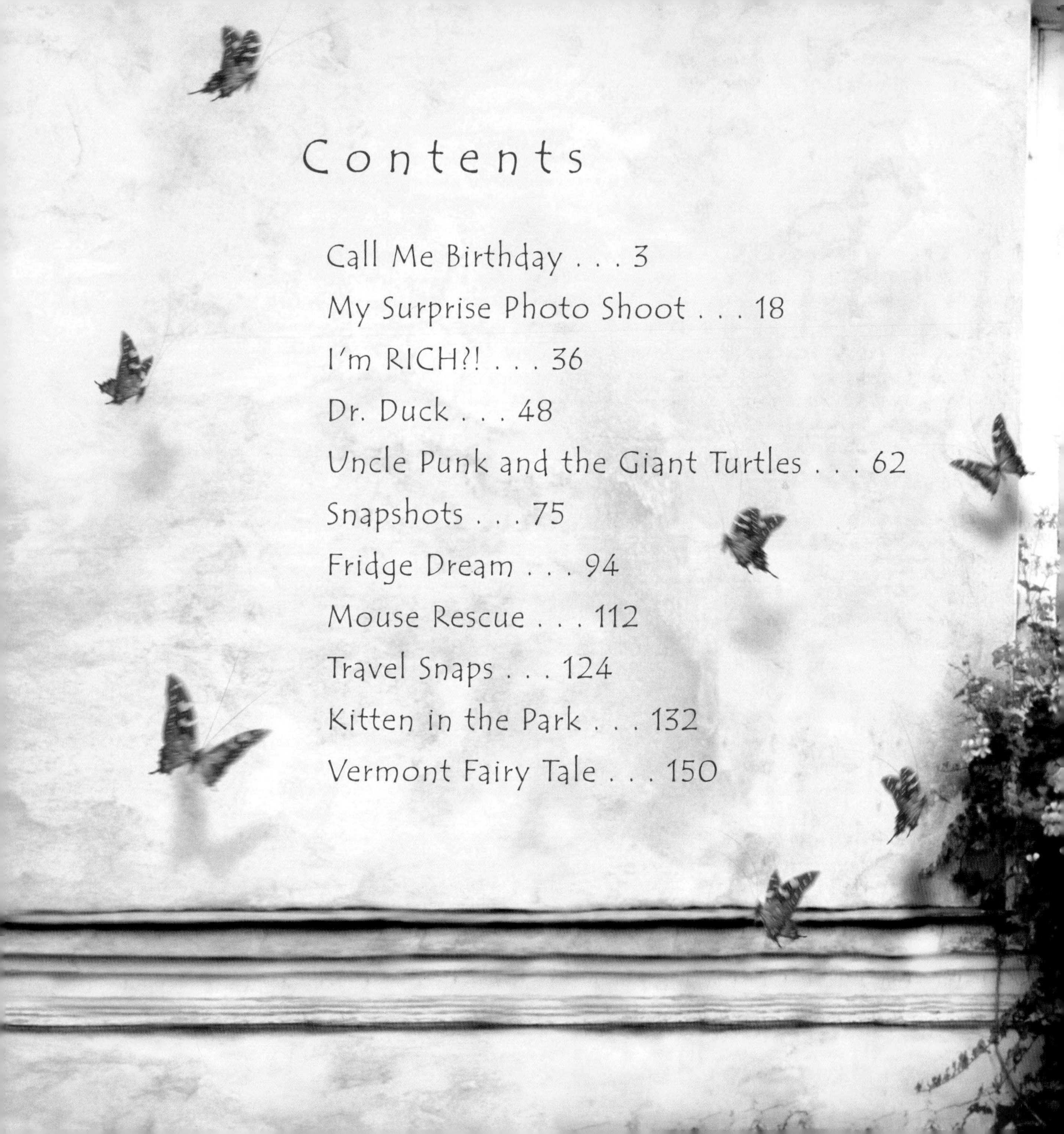

Contents

Call Me Birthday . . . 3

My Surprise Photo Shoot . . . 18

I'm RICH?! . . . 36

Dr. Duck . . . 48

Uncle Punk and the Giant Turtles . . . 62

Snapshots . . . 75

Fridge Dream . . . 94

Mouse Rescue . . . 112

Travel Snaps . . . 124

Kitten in the Park . . . 132

Vermont Fairy Tale . . . 150

Happy
Birthday,
the Cat

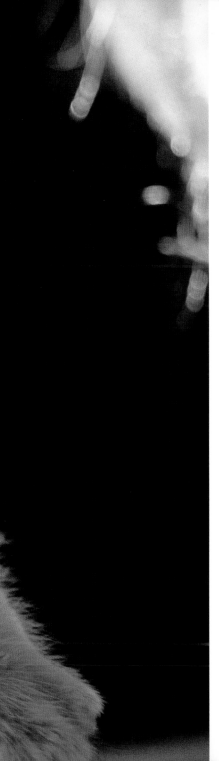

Call Me Birthday

It was spring when I was born. Some kind neighbors in Little Italy found my brothers and sisters and me on the street, but they already had so many cats at home, they put us in a vacant store window with the sign "Looking for a home. Will work for food."

Hi! I'm Birthday.

3

We crawled around and saw lots of people looking at us from the street side of the glass. Within a few days, I was taken to a nice family, but they found out that one of them was allergic to cats and soon I was back in the window again. All of my brothers and sisters had gone to new homes, and I was all by myself looking at people passing by. It was so lonely, with nobody to snuggle or talk to, I just sat there alone and cried, "Meow, meow."

Baby me

On a beautiful April Sunday afternoon, I was sitting in the window bathed in sparkling spring sunlight when I felt somebody watching me. I looked up through my tears, and I spotted a pretty lady staring at me with binoculars from one of the many windows across the street. My, she had big eyes. I tried very hard to look as cute as possible so she would bring me home. I wiped my tears, smiled, stretched, flipped, and waved my tail up in the air to let her know I was looking at her, too. She moved from one window to the next, standing behind window boxes filled with pink and red flowers, watching me all the time.

I pictured myself in her window surrounded by fragrant flowers and butterflies, looking out at the world. While my imagination took over, I lost track of her. Where was she?

I couldn't see her in the window anymore. I looked for her in all of the windows, then suddenly here she was! I saw her standing right in front of me looking through the glass. I smiled and stuck my tail straight up in the air. I liked her right away because she had a long, thick, dark tail on the back of her head. She came into the dark store, and my heart was pounding so hard, I could hear it like the bell at the church nearby.

She slowly picked me up in her warm hands. I felt purring-good. This must be what they call love at first sight. She handled me like a frail bird in an eggshell and moved me to a man's hands. At first, I was worried because I could not find any tail on the back of his head, but soon I noticed that his short hair was mixed colors and very similar to mine.

"Happy Birthday!" Papa said to Mama with a loving smile. I was passed from his big hands back to Mama's palms. She held me against her soft chest, and I heard her delighted voice: "My best birthday present!" She was ecstatic.

I was so HAPPY!

I arrived at my new home with my loving parents.

The whole world is within my reach!

Mama put me down on a big carpet warmed by the afternoon sun streaming through the window. I slowly marched around all over the warm carpet, but I was a little bit afraid to go beyond the edge. I listened carefully to hear if anybody was sneezing. No, they were just giggling. Papa brought me warm milk in a bottle. I realized I was hungry after all the excitement. While I drank the tasty milk,

Mama asked Papa, "What should we call her?"

I opened my eyes and thought, "I am Happy Birthday." My new Papa must have read my mind because he said, "Call her Birthday, because today is your birthday, and it is her birthday, too."

That's how I became Birthday.

My first big step—climbing Papa's boots

14

Always salute your superior.

My Surprise Photo Shoot

This is my first official studio portrait. The day it was taken was memorable. For the sitting, I had to take a bath in the morning. I thought I could take care of myself and that I was clean enough. But my parents wanted me to be a fluffy, puffy, shining star. I told Mama she could only wash my whiskers. She didn't listen.

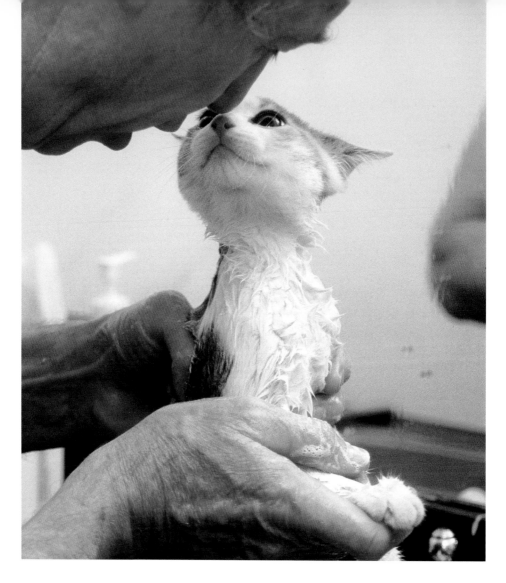

I was put in a sink with a little bit of warm water. Papa held me with his big hands while Mama poured pink cat shampoo slowly on my paws, tail, back, belly, neck, and head. Papa's hands moved all over my wet and soapy body, tickling me. He could reach my body where my tongue couldn't, so I started to think, "Maybe this bath isn't so bad."

Then I looked at myself in the mirror. "Oh, my goodness!" I looked like a space creature. My surprise didn't stop there. When Papa poured water over me, I thought all of my fur would melt away down the drain, so I started to panic. Both Papa and Mama tried to calm me down, but I couldn't hear what they were saying.

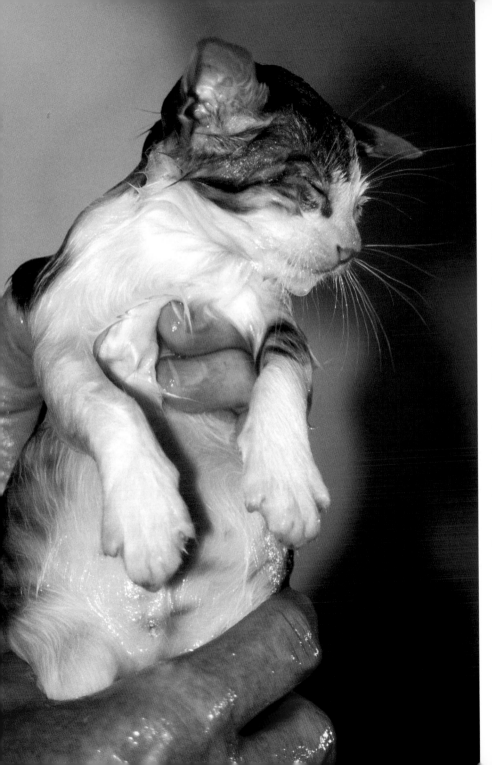

I was almost crying, but I was afraid my tears would melt my eyes, and I kept them closed. I was sure I would start to disappear. Everything was soaking wet and melting and so was my brain. I felt like I was back in my cat mummy's big tummy being pushed softly against my brothers and sisters. The warmth of their bodies made me feel so very good. Then all of a sudden I was thrown into a storm with heavy rain. I felt cold and knew I was out of the womb. I opened my eyes and burst out crying.

Papa and Mama kept changing towels to dry my fur. I couldn't stop meowing. Warm air from a dryer with a screaming noise helped to fluff my wet fur back to normal, and I calmed down. When I was finally dry, Mama combed my fur from head to tail. Being a model is not easy, you know. Later, I ate special snacks that Papa gave me, then took a nap.

My sweet, bubbly dream after my bath

When I woke up,
the brightness of
my white belly
almost blinded me.
Papa gave me a new
red collar with a
shiny red bell. When
I scratched the back of
my ears, the bell rang.
When I ran, it rang some
more. That made me happy.
Papa put me on his shoulder, and
we went upstairs to the studio. He
put me down on a white table and turned
the music on. The lights were already in position
for me, so Papa turned on the modeling lights and
Mama turned off the overhead lights. The shooting began.

Papa took some Polaroid shots to check the exposure, and Mama brushed me again and wiped the fallen hairs off the white table. I was like a fluffy, puffy movie star on a set with spotlights all around me. I liked it! I started posing with a big red ball. I rested my right paw on it, looked to the right, then to the left, and moved my pink nose up and down. The red bell rang and rang. Every time I moved, the flash popped and then came the sound of the strobe recharging. Mama and Papa both worked the lights, positioning them at different angles to emphasize my cuteness. I knew what to do because I had seen the pretty models move around in the lights for fashion shoots. I was only wearing the red collar, so it was not too difficult to pose. I liked the red ball that matched my ring-ring bell. When we were in the middle of our shoot, we had visitors.

Who are you?

One of the newcomers was Cao Yong, the painter whom Papa had met in Tibet. Cao is a high-energy man, and I could feel his power radiating all around his strong body. At first I thought he talked funny, and then I saw a little bird whose feathers were painted green, gray, and yellow talking on his shoulder. Big Cao spoke tenderly and lovingly to his little buddy. "Topi, say hi to Birthday."

Topi was a parakeet. He moved sideways to get on Cao's thick index finger with paint under the nail. Cao softly put Topi down right next to me on the white light table. Now I could clearly see painted orange circles on his cheeks. Everyone was looking at him.

Topi whistled to me and started walking on the table. I had thought I was the center of the universe until he showed up. Now I had to share the spotlight with the orange-cheek-paint-bird!

Papa started photographing me and Topi together. I walked to left; he walked to right. He walked forward; I turned back. When we moved apart, Papa told me to get close to Topi. So I turned around. Topi did, too. I had never seen a parakeet before. He was actually kind of cute with his orange cheeks, but I didn't want to get close to him because I was afraid his paint might rub off on me. When both of us were back in the center of the table, I asked Topi with curiosity, "What is the real color of your feathers?"

Topi looked at me and said, "These are my real feathers. Let me show you my wings." He spread his wings right in front of my eyes and fluttered them. I closed my eyes with surprise as the strong breeze swept over me. When I opened my eyes, Topi was sitting on top of Cao's head and whistling. The shoot was done because everyone was doubled over laughing and couldn't stop. I was puzzled about what was so funny. I was just trying not to get green paint on me because I didn't want to take a bath again.

Later that week, when I went into the computer room to take my daily catnap on the big warm monitor, I was shocked to see the picture on the screen—Topi with a big grin on his orange-cheeked face right next to me! Such an insult. I didn't even want to tell you. It was supposed to be a pretty picture of me, instead I looked like chicken. Well, this is only a story. Not true, not true!

Who is that?

I'm RICH?!

I t was a hot, sticky New York summer afternoon, and our studio was very dark and quiet. All the windows were covered up, and no boiling-hot sunlight came through. No crazy traffic noise or festive music rose from the street below. There was only the steady sound of the air conditioner vibrating in the dark and keeping us cool.

Mama and Papa were busy in the studio setting up lights for a photo shoot. As usual, I brought my rolly ball to Papa to play. When he hears my rolly ball drop, he always stops

what he is doing and picks it up with a big smile. As soon as I see the ball slip into his hand, I turn around and anxiously wait for him to throw it. I stick my ears up like antennae and listen for the first tinkling noise of the ball so I know which direction to run. He always says, "Rolly ball!" and teases me a little. I must be ready when he throws it. I wait for a short moment with all of my muscles tensed up like an Olympic sprinter at the starting line. I'm like a coiled spring. The studio is a big open space with a highly polished floor. My small ball rolls around from wall to wall like a bullet. When the silver bullet leaves Papa's hand, I hit the floor with my back feet slipping and sliding and go bananas chasing the ball. I grab it in my mouth, bring it back to Papa, and he throws it again. That's our game. I also like it when he throws the ball down the long steps. Running down to chase the ball, I skip many steps. I run fast even though I have to watch out not to crash into the glass door at the bottom. Nobody in our house goes up and down the steps as quick as I can. But on this hot afternoon, Mama and Papa were so involved with what they were doing that Papa threw the ball for me only once. So I kicked it around and played with it by myself.

Finally, I got bored and thought, "Last kick!" *Crack, crack, crack.* The ball rolled, I chased. When I ended up in the middle of the room, I saw an old, battered silver attaché case full of money in the spotlight. I dropped the little silver ball in shock. I had never seen so much money. I was excited but curious. "Who gave me this money? How much is there?" Questions buzzed around in my brain. "How many cans of cat food can I buy? I bet it's more than Papa can carry—my lifetime supply or more! Of course, I have nine lives. Maybe it's not enough." I looked around and realized that nobody was in the studio. I sniffed at the money. They were real hundred-dollar bills. Smelled like thousands of them. I quickly marked them to claim they were mine. Then I looked for Mama and Papa. Where did they go? I had such exciting news to tell

them. I was afraid to leave the money, so I waited inside the case protecting it for them. I got inside and closed the lid. I usually fall asleep after running with my rolly ball, but I was so excited about the money, my eyes were wide open in the darkness. Smelling the ink on the bills, I imagined so many wild thoughts. What would I do with this sudden fortune? What could I buy beside cat food? How about a big field full of mint! Oh, mint! My favorite flavor. The thought was so exciting, I could even smell the mint in the box. Twitching my nose, I thought about traveling around the world to taste gourmet cat food. I had always wanted to go to Venice. I pictured myself in a pretty Venetian dress with a red feathered hat, having a nap in a gondola and romantically floating down a canal.

Hide the money.

Instead of Venetian boat songs, I heard footsteps. I tensed my body, listening carefully to hear who it might be. I knew it wasn't Mama, and it sounded like Papa's cowboy boots. I thought I could buy him a new pair. Black or brown? Well, maybe both. The boots stopped right in front of me. I held my breath, hoping it was Papa. I was so anxious, my pink nose was sweating. It was hot in the money case. The lid lifted half open, and before I could see Papa's face, pow! the bright white flash of light almost knocked me out. Papa and Mama's laughing voices brought me back. I said, "I found a lot of money!" I jumped out of the attaché case and started to tell them about my amazing discovery. Then I heard other footsteps coming up to the studio. Who were they? I told Papa, "Hide this money!" and closed the lid and sat on top of the case. Two men in black uniforms, who looked like policemen, came in with a big black dog. The dog winked at me, barked loud, and said, "Thank you for protecting the money."

I jumped up and gave the dog my meanest face, but it was in vain. The two men shook hands with Papa, grabbed my silver case full of money, and left the studio. The big dog followed. It happened in the blink of an eye. I was so shocked, I couldn't move until Mama opened the shutters and raised a window. A streak of sunlight beamed into the white studio.

I turned to Papa and cried, "Why did you give MY money to the dog people?"

"Was that YOUR money? How did you earn it?" Papa asked while he put his equipment away.

I thought for a moment, then answered with confidence, "I found it."

"Well, you must earn it to make it yours. Marking it isn't enough." He laughed.

I was puzzled. "How can I earn it?"

"You work hard, make people happy, and you stay happy," Papa replied with a big smile.

Work? Me? Well, I turned around and found my rolly ball sparkling in the sun. I bit it and was glad they didn't take it with the money. I would be very upset if I lost my favorite rolly ball. "Papa, let's play!" I dropped my rolly ball on Papa's boot.

See you later, money.

Dr. Duck

When I smell coffee in the morning, I know it's time for my breakfast. Papa serves me before Mama serves him. While they are eating, I go to the potty. Then Papa and I play with my rolly ball while he drinks his second cup of coffee. One morning, Papa disappeared as soon as he finished his first cup. Mama was washing dishes when I came out from my potty. I asked, "Where is Papa?"

"He went out to get Dr. Duck. They should be back soon."

I sat on the steps and waited, staring at the front door. Aunt Yumiko, who was visiting from Japan, opened the door and came up the steps.

"Hi, Birthday. What are you doing here?" she asked.

"I'm waiting for Dr. Duck and Papa!"

"Are you sick?"

"No."

"Is your Papa sick?"

"No."

"I know your Mama isn't sick. Who is Dr. Duck coming to see?"

"I don't know."

Aunt Yumiko sat next to me curiously. She stroked my back telling me about Shima and Sakura, my Japanese cousins, when Papa opened the front door. We both jumped up because a foul smell filled our hallway. Papa was carrying a big box and something inside it was making a funny noise. He had both of his arms stretched out as much as possible so he could keep the box away from his nose. The smell had already reached Mama, who came out from her office with fingers pinching her nose. Before she could complain, Papa said, "Bring shampoo and towels! I have to give Dr. Duck a bath."

Aunt Yumiko and I looked at each other. "Who is Dr. Duck?"

Waiting for Dr. Duck

Me and Dr. Duck. Quack! Quack!

Papa walked directly to the bathroom, and Mama, Aunt Yumiko, and I followed. Papa took most of his clothes off, then opened the mystery box on the floor in front of the shower. A pair of filthy white wings appeared and scattered dirty fuzzy feathers, followed by a yellow beak quacking loud. Dr. Duck was a stinky bird!

I jumped onto Aunt Yumiko's shoulder to take a good look at this unusual event of Papa giving a shower to a duck! It was funny to watch half-naked Papa and the quacky duck take a shower together. Papa poured shampoo over the duck's feathers, scrubbed him very well, and rinsed. He repeated it many times. The duck was very excited. He quacked a lot and stretched and shook his big wings, splashing soapy water on Papa's face. Every time he opened his wings, I could see that he was getting cleaner, and soon the only smell in the room was of Mama's shampoo. Papa was wet as a goose when he came out of the shower with Dr. Duck. Mama put towels around both of them and soon they were clean and dry.

"Let Dr. Duck march around the studio for a while until he gets used to it," Papa said. We all gathered and watched Dr. Duck travel back and forth the whole length of the white studio, while Papa described how dreadful the place was where Dr. Duck lived before.

Papa had found Dr. Duck at an old Chinese poultry store. It was a filthy, smelly, small, dark place filled with poultry cages stacked from floor to ceiling, wall to wall, like little prison cells. Each cage was filled with about fifteen birds packed in like sardines with no way to stretch their wings. Most were born in the poultry barns and never had a chance to walk under the sun. What a terrible life they had! Papa told a man at the store that he needed a duck. The man stuck his arms into one of the cages and struggled with the frantically resisting birds. Finally, he grabbed a duck by the neck and pulled it out. He asked Papa with a squeaky voice, "Do you need the neck, too?" Hearing such an unexpected question, Papa realized he was an unusual customer. This was a store that supplied Peking ducks for Chinese restaurants. Papa had to tell the man repeatedly he needed a live duck. Finally, Dr. Duck was shoved into a box. Papa paid the man and left the stinky place carrying Dr. Duck.

I looked at this lucky duck with amazement and wondered how he could have become a doctor under those conditions. He seemed to be calming down, and soon he started to relax. He slowly walked toward me, and he spoke as if he could read my mind. "I studied very hard to become a doctor."

"Where did you study?" I asked skeptically. Here is the story he told me.

The lucky duck was born in a small village in China. When he was still little and playing with his brothers, he fell in a river. He struggled, but the water ran too fast, and he was washed away. He showed me his scarred toe and told how he had bumped a rock in the rapids and injured it. He managed to float for a long time, and then he was too tired to think anymore. Finally, somebody picked him out of the water and stuffed him in a bag. The exhausted baby duck slept all the way to the home of the young man who had picked him up, a medical student. The lucky duck started to learn about medicine because the student read aloud from his medical books. Then the young man decided to come to America. Mr. Duck hid in the young man's suitcase and read all the young man's medicine books during the long journey. When he found out Mr. Duck was in his suitcase, the young man was very upset and tried to give him to the cook on the ship. The almost unlucky duck begged the young man not to and told him all the things he knew about medicine. The student was very impressed and decided to spare him. They studied together in their little cabin, hidden from the other passengers. When they finally arrived in America, Mr. Lucky Duck told the young man they had to go through immigration and customs separately. Otherwise, the young man might be arrested for bringing a live animal into the country. So Mr. Duck jumped into a cage with chickens and ducks. It was an awful choice, but he knew it was too late to go back. He saw that many of his kind were sick and weak. So, he began to take care of sick birds. He told me all the life stories the birds told him, about their physical pains and emotional trials. His cage ended up at the poultry market. "When I was grabbed out of the cage, I closed my eyes and thought, 'This is it. My career is over.' Then your papa told the man in the store, 'No chopping!' I couldn't believe I was alive. Your Papa told me I was going to be Dr. Duck, so I said, 'I AM Dr. Duck!' Your Papa is lucky to find me. I am the real Dr. Duck. You know, it's hard to find the right doctor when you need one."

What a scary story! I was sorry for him, but I thought that he was the lucky one to find Papa. Anyway, the fact that he was alive and out of the stinky place made me happy. I knew how terrible it was because I thought I would die just smelling him when he arrived.

Papa used his favorite quote: "What you are seeking is seeking you. That's how nature fulfills itself. Let's start shooting."

"Shooting?!" Dr. Duck hollered.

I came up to Papa and whispered, "Don't say *shooting*—ducks get scared when they hear that word."

Papa put Dr. Duck on the top of a white box and started photographing him. He was a very good model. I was quite impressed with the way he posed. First I thought he would fall off the box, but that's why Mama and Aunt Yumiko were standing on both sides. When Papa said, "Turn right," Dr. Duck turned to Aunt Yumiko and winked. When Papa said, "Turn left," Dr. Duck looked at Mama and quacked. The shoot went very smoothly.

While Papa and Mama were putting the equipment away, Dr. Duck asked, "What is the picture for?"

They looked at each other and hesitated. Then Papa said, "This photo is going on the cover of a magazine."

Dr. Duck asked curiously, "Which one?"

Papa explained that a few days ago, an art director from a medical magazine called to discuss a cover illustration for their next issue. The main article was about bogus doctors on the

Internet, and Papa came up with the idea of a quack doctor.

Dr. Duck was totally puzzled and leaned his head down to me, "Why me as a bogus doctor? I'm a good doctor!"

I looked to Aunt Yumiko for the answer. She spoke with her Japanese accent. "I don't really know. I guess that must be an English expression."

Mama looked at Papa and said, "You'd better explain *quack doctor* to Dr. Duck."

When Dr. Duck heard that quack meant a fake doctor, he went berserk and

chased me all over the place quacking, "Come here, Birthday. Quack! I'm going to examine you. Quack!"

Papa, Mama, and Aunt Yumiko tried to keep us apart. He was so annoying, I told him, "Leave me alone or I will make Peking duck out of you!" I had to punch him to keep him away from me. He quacked and calmed down.

Mama told him that he should not take it personally. He breathed deeply and nodded. He asked Papa how he could find his dear friend whom he had lost at immigration. The young man wanted to become a pediatrician, so Papa suggested that Dr. Duck work at a children's petting zoo. There he could ask the children if they knew the young doctor. Papa called a zoo and arranged a job for Dr. Duck. After a week, he left us. We wished him good luck for his new journey.

Dr. Duck now lives and works in the petting zoo, having a good time with children and other animals. I don't know if he ever found the young man or not, but he has a happy life with a lot of friends. Mama and Papa visit Dr. Duck every time they go to the zoo. I would, too, but I'm not allowed there.

Everyone has his own story to tell friends. Tell me about your red eyes.

Uncle Punk and the Giant Turtles

Sometimes, Mama and Papa go away for a while, and I stay in the studio with Uncle Punk. He is a famous artist and is always busy working, but he pays attention to me and plays with me. When I want to play, I usually come up and talk to Uncle Punk. "Meow!" He looks down and thinks *meow* means, "I'm hungry," so he goes downstairs to the kitchen and opens a big can of cat food and puts it in my dish. He feeds me a lot more than Papa and Mama. To please Uncle Punk, I eat it. When he sees me finish, he goes back to work. Then later, when I come up to say, "Uncle Punk, let's play. Meow!" he says, "You, Punk! Are you hungry again?" He always calls me Punk, and that's why I call him Uncle Punk. He runs downstairs and feeds me again. This goes on two or three times a day. I get tired from eating so I have to lie down a lot. When I get up, Uncle Punk thinks I'm hungry, and he feeds me again. Then he runs out of cat food and mumbles, "Your mama and papa never leave

Meow!
I'm hungry.

62

enough food for you." He goes out to buy more. By the time Mama and Papa come home, I am really fat. Uncle Punk tells them, "Oh, I didn't feed her except when she was hungry."

Uncle Punk thinks I'm psychic because I know when Mama and Papa are coming home. I get messages in my brain, a clear vision of Mama and Papa opening the front door and calling, "Birthday!" I go and sit on a step on the second floor where I can look all the way down to the front door. Sometimes I wait two or three hours, sometimes ten minutes. I don't know the difference between three hours and ten minutes because I can't tell time. It all seems the same to me because I fall asleep waiting. Then, Papa puts me on his shoulder and we go into our apartment together. I get big hugs and kisses and they feed me. I'm so happy they are home.

Flower power

When I was young, we had two small turtles in an aquarium. Their names were Kinsan and Ginsan (Gold and Silver) after famous Japanese twin sisters who had celebrated their 100th birthday. Our Kinsan and Ginsan invited me to their water home a few times, but I don't like water. We played together every week when they came out of their aquarium while Papa cleaned it. Papa said, "Birthday, take good care of them while I wash their home." When they were out of the water, they moved very slowly. But they were sneaky and ran off in different directions. I had to tell them to stay close. I would tell Kinsan to stop, then Ginsan to turn around. They understood what I said. I liked playing with them on the floor.

I know a funny story about our turtles and Uncle Punk. One night, Mama and Papa met an old Chinese woman who had two much-larger turtles. She said, "I am looking for someone to take the turtles because I am moving tomorrow and they can't go with me. I'll have to dump them on the street if I can't find a home for them. I have no other choice."

My mama and papa looked at each other and said, "Oh, well, we'll take them." So they brought the new turtles home, and I came up with a great idea. I looked up at Papa and he made a big grin. He winked and said, "That's a funny idea, Birthday." We decided to play a big joke on Uncle Punk.

The next day, Uncle Punk came into the studio, and he and Papa worked as usual. Mama came running upstairs screaming, "Papa! Uncle Punk! Come down quick! Something terrible happened to our little turtles." We all ran to see the turtles. We looked in the aquarium, where the two big turtles were swimming in the water. Mama had put the new, big turtles in the aquarium and hid little Kinsan and Ginsan. Uncle Punk's eyes popped out of his head, and I thought they might fall in the water. "Holy cow! What happened to Kinsan and Ginsan?" he yelled.

"I don't know. Papa made a crazy new food the other day, and he has been feeding it to them. It must have made them swell up," Mama said.

Uncle Punk's eyes got even bigger. "Hey, I've been eating the same food,

Boy, my parents are very good actors.

and I've been feeling good and strong. It was protein powder and vitamin pills. Your husband has been eating it, too!"

Mama exclaimed, "You two are crazy! Look what happened to the turtles!"

Boy! She was a pretty good actor, and I was impressed. Uncle Punk's face got really puzzled, and he started sweating. He muttered, "What's going on?" Then he turned around to Papa and said, "You should call the Animal Medical Center."

Papa also made a puzzled face, opened the thick, heavy phone book, found the number, and called. He pushed the speaker phone and we all sat listening.

"Animal Medical Center. May I help you?" a woman answered.

Papa said politely, "I need a herpetologist. My green turtles are having a problem."

The operator said, "Hold on, please."

Waiting music came on. No one talked, and soon someone picked up the line. Papa acted anxious and picked up the telephone receiver, which automatically turned off the speaker phone. I saw him disconnect the line at the same time, but Uncle Punk did not see that. Papa is a good actor. Now, he pretended to talk to a herpetologist, saying, "Oh, our little turtles doubled in size just overnight! We have been feeding them special food with protein and vitamins." Then he waited and listened. We all kept quiet. Papa cried, "What do you mean? That's terrible. What should we do? Okay, Okay, we won't touch them. Yes, we won't even touch the food. We'll wait for your call back. Thank you, doctor." He said, "Talk to you soon," and hung up.

"What did the doctor say?" Uncle Punk asked Papa right away.

Papa took a deep breath, then said, "Well, the doctor said he never heard of anything like this, but he'll discuss it with a turtle specialist and call us back this afternoon. He said we shouldn't touch the turtles or the food they've been eating because that may have caused this unusual event, and it might be contagious to humans."

I looked at Uncle Punk—he was turning blue. I thought he was going to pass out. He looked at me and said, "I think Birthday is swelling up or else she is getting fat in a hurry." Then he questioned Papa in low voice, "You fed the terrible mystery food to Birthday, didn't you?"

"No, she wouldn't eat it."

"Smart Punk."

Uncle Punk mumbled and went back to the studio. We burst out laughing. I ran back to our bathroom to tell Kinsan and Ginsan about Uncle Punk. They were floating peacefully in the red bathtub. When I explained to them about how puzzled Uncle Punk was, they giggled and moved their little tails in the water. I told them to keep quiet. Uncle Punk came down to our apartment every thirty minutes or so to check on the mysterious turtles. He was sure that they were getting bigger right before his eyes. He would ask Papa, "Has the doctor called back yet?" and look at his watch anxiously.

How are you doing? Are you getting big yet?

Giantism?

When the phone in our kitchen rang at about one o'clock in the afternoon, we all ran to it and Mama picked up. She made sure Uncle Punk was nearby, then pushed the speaker on the phone. A man's voice said, "Hi, I'm Dr. J. I am a herpetologist specializing in giantism, a new disease your turtles might have."

Dr. J is Papa's close friend from Brooklyn. He's not a real doctor, of course, but Papa asked him to join our practical joke on Uncle Punk. Dr. J went on, "Giantism is a mysterious disease that only occurs in green turtles in a small contained area. It is highly contagious to all other turtles, other pets that you have in your house, and even to us humans. If any of you in your family are feeling tired, headachy, sweaty, have swelling in the hands, or any unusual symptoms, don't wait— go to the emergency room right away and get a shot for giantism. We have reports of death caused by this new disease. I will come to your house at four o'clock and take your turtles to be examined. Don't touch them."

Mama told Dr. J how to get to our place, thanked him, then hung up the phone. Uncle Punk was pale and sweating. I thought he would faint. He spoke with a frail voice. "Do you think Dr. J can take care of humans, too? I have a headache, but I don't want to go to the emergency room."

An hour later, Uncle Punk came downstairs to our apartment again, but this time he shouted, "Holy cow!" He jumped a couple of feet, ran without touching the floor, and brought back Mama and Papa, saying, "Look, now they are shrinking!"

Oh, how terrible we are. There were Kinsan and Ginsan back in the tank swimming innocently. The big ones were hidden in the bathtub. "I have to sit down." Totally puzzled, Uncle Punk went back to the studio and tried to breathe normally. I followed him and sat right next to him. He looked at me and asked, "Are you going to miss me when I am gone? I should go to the emergency room."

At that moment, Mama yelled again. We ran downstairs to the aquarium, and there were four turtles swimming peacefully. Uncle Punk's mouth dropped open and no word came out. Papa said, "This is a severe case of multiplicity!" Uncle Punk gave the three of us a real dirty look.

Uncle Punk wouldn't speak to us for a week.

Ha! Ha! Ha! We got Uncle Punk.

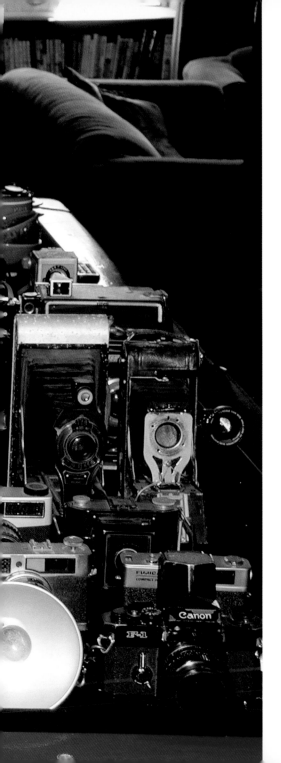

Snapshots

Which one is the meow key?

Children,
   don't try this
      at home.

Parents,
   don't try this
      with your children!

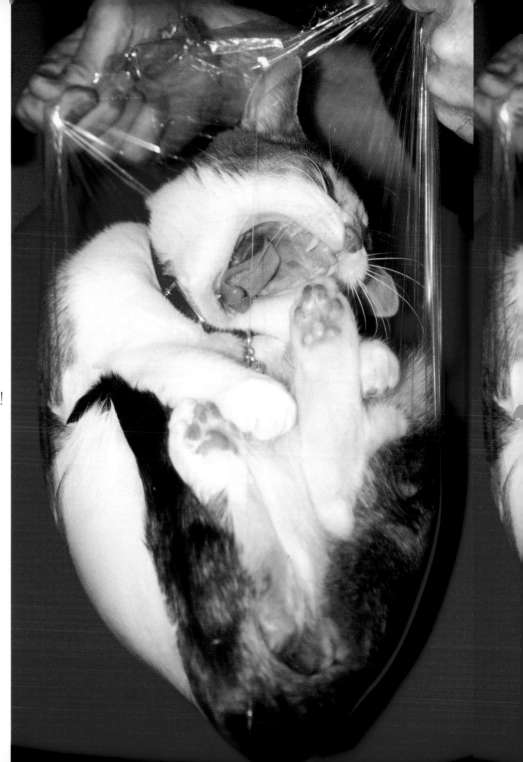

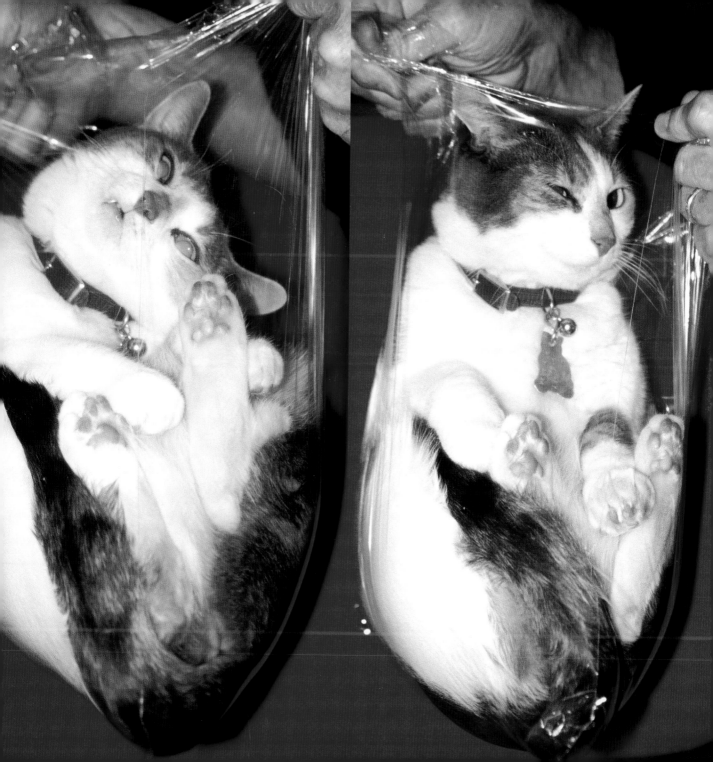

Papa helps to stretch my back.

I scratch Papa's back.

How come I don't get a mouse with my computer?

Do I look
like you?

Big smooch to my bear friend

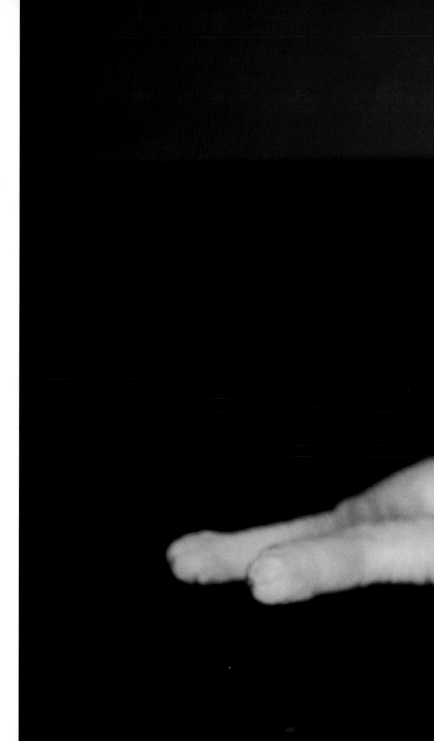

If I tell you my secret,
    will you give me the fish?

Aim!   Attack!

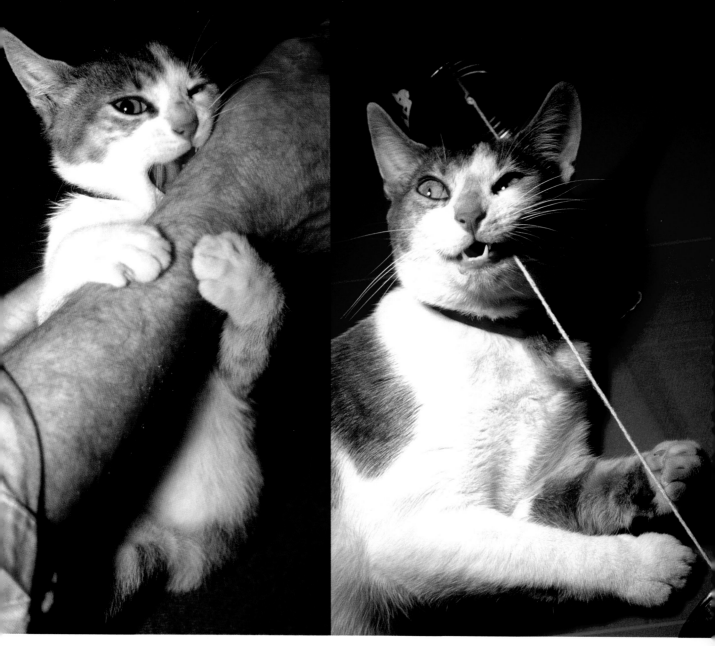

Attack!   Floss after every attack!

Always know
   your exit strategy.

Fridge Dream

One day, Mama and Papa bought a big new refrigerator. It came in the biggest box I had ever seen, and three big men carried it up the stairs to our kitchen. When the shiny white refrigerator was taken out of the box, our phone rang and Papa answered it. He talked to his agent while Mama directed the men to where to install the big white fridge. I sniffed an orange fish-shaped logo on the empty big brown box discarded on the floor. Then I jumped in. Inside, the box was warm and comfortable. I curled up, closed my eyes, and listened to Papa talking about photographing a movie star's house in Bel Air, California. He described a luxury house with many elegant rooms, swimming pools, and beautiful flower gardens with statues and fountains. It sounded so beautiful that I could smell the pink roses in the garden.

I started to enjoy the fantasy of being in this extraordinary house. . . .

The people who own it say I can walk around without a leash, so I start exploring. I walk on white marble floors that are cold on my paws. I come to a flowery-patterned red carpet, then a green-and-white marble floor that goes on and on and on. After I pass several big doors, a tasty smell reaches my nose. I follow it and arrive at a big kitchen with a lot of pots and pans hanging in the center. A lady with a white apron sees me, gives me a warm smile, then cuts a piece of salmon pâté for me. It is heavenly. I stay in the kitchen and watch the woman work hard until she finally sits down and falls asleep after eating a big sandwich for lunch. I have another bite of salmon pâté from the table before I leave the kitchen and start marching again. I walk from room to room to room, and each one is tastefully decorated with beautiful furniture. I come to a room with many books, and jump up on a big desk by a window to look out. The window is closed, but warm sunlight is pouring into the room through the glass. All of a sudden, I realize I have to go to the potty.

So, I jump off the desk and start looking. "Potty, potty, potty, where is the potty? Is anybody there? Tell me where to go?" Nobody is around. The ceiling of the corridor is so high, it hurts my neck to look up. I deep-sniff to catch the smell of a potty, but there is none. So I stick my ears up high and slowly turn around to hear any potty noise. I hear leaves whispering in the wind, and I start moving in that direction. As I get closer, I can hear flowers singing songs. The melody makes me happier and happier, and my steps get lighter and faster. An unmistakable whiff of earthy fresh dirt touches my nose. I find many trees and flowers in a beautiful room with a glass ceiling. It is filled with warm sun, and all the plants are exquisite. There is a giant old stone fountain carved with angels and birds in the middle of the room. It's like being in heaven. I feel so welcome, and I step on the red, earthy tiled floor. A soft voice speaks to me. "Come, Birthday. Water me." I turn and see a beautiful pink flower smiling at me. So, I do. "If you think like a queen, poop like a queen!"

As I am covering up, out comes a butler. When he sees me in the pot, he yells at me. "What are you doing in there? Bad cat!" He scares me so much, I can hardly finish what I am doing, and I jump out of the flowerpot. He starts chasing me, so I start running. I run right out a door, across a great lawn, past a couple of swimming pools and the tennis court, dash into the woods, and jump the old stone wall. Then I run down a road, but I don't know where I am going. When I stop running from the butler, I am out of breath. Suddenly, I realize I'm lost. I don't know where I am. I sit down to calm myself; I lick my paws. Along comes a mail truck, and a man gets out to deliver some letters. I walk up to him. "Meow! I'm Birthday, and I'm lost." He looks down and says, "Hi, Birthday, would you like a ride?" He picks me up and puts me on the seat next to him. I see big bags full of letters in the back, and I ask him, "Can you take me to my home?"

"Sorry, I can't. I have to deliver all of these letters."

"If I put a stamp on my face, can you deliver me home like a letter?"

"You need an address to deliver a letter. Do you know your address?"

I look down. Oh, my goodness! My name tag with my address and phone number is gone. I must have dropped it when I was running. I am sad and quiet because I don't know my address. The mailman keeps driving, stopping here and there to drop off the mail. It's a long ride, so I snooze. When the last bag of letters rolls out of the back of the truck, we are at a beach. The mailman says, "That's it, Birthday. I've finished today's delivery, and I'm going home. I can't take you to my home because I have a dog who is afraid of cats."

I thank him for the ride, and I hop out of the mail truck.

Beach! The wind picks up my loose fur, and it flies away into the salty air. I look around, and I am scared. I have never seen such a big potty. What kind of creature uses this vast sand beach for his potty? This must be a giant's potty. I am very scared. I look for a place to hide, but there is nothing. I move a few steps and stop. I look around again, take a few more steps, then lie flat on the sand. I have never seen waves before. I stare at them for a while. They never stop moving. Finally, I see a pier over by the big ocean. My instinct tells me to go there. I run, but it takes forever because my feet sink into the sand. I am out of breath and very tired by the time I arrive under the pier. The sun is floating in the ocean and painting everything in orange. The wind dies down. I feel better the moment I look at the sunset. It's dark under the pier, but there are so many interesting smells. I like this place. A spark of orange light catches my attention. I see the little orange fish logo from a refrigerator crate reflecting in the last glint of sunlight. I walk over to the big brown box and sniff the orange fish with my little but powerful nose. It smells like home. This is a nice big box to sleep in. It comes with a view of the ocean. Feeling the cool evening sea breeze on my face, I rub my whiskered cheeks to mark on the refrigerator box. This is mine! I am so excited and proud of myself as I enter my new home. I step into the box, but then I jump out immediately. Somebody is in the box!

I lie as flat as I can on the sand, feeling its dampness on my white belly. I hold still and watch the man in the box come out. The box

shakes, and his long bearded face sticks out. He looks around to find me. I can smell ocean in his long yellow hair when he shakes his head. His tanned muscular shoulders and arms pop out of the box, and salty sand sprinkles on me. He comes out of the box like a giant genie appearing from a magic lamp. He looks and smells like he needs a bath badly. I don't move. I bury half of my body and face in the sand and look up at him with just my eyes. He finds me and leans over with his big body. "Hello, kitty. What is your name?" he asks with tender strokes on my back.

"My name is Birthday." My voice trembles, but I'm not afraid of him. I'm just shocked.

"Mine is DC." He smiles.

I like him right away. As I feel relief, my empty belly growls for attention. "Hi, DC. Do you have anything to eat?"

He looks down at me and says, "You bet. Come on, Birthday." He walks toward the ocean. I follow him, but I am so slow, he turns back and picks me up. I feel a lot safer in his warm arms.

Me and DC go off down the beach, and DC starts digging in the sand as if he needs to go to the potty. I watch him, not wanting to disturb his

business, and soon the hole starts filling with water. I'm puzzled, because I did not see him peeing in there. When did he pee? He is a strange man. He keeps digging and digging. Finally, he sticks his hands in the big wet sand hole and pulls out a handful of wet sand. He dumps it on a wooden board and separates out sand and tiny red creatures. They are very funny looking.

"These are sand crabs." DC breaks them open and he puts them in his mouth. I sniff them first, and then I lick them. They are very tasty, but sandy-crunchy. I eat one; DC eats one. I eat two; DC eats two. We eat more, and finally we eat them all. Sand crabs are so tasty! I would like to give some of these sand crabs to the lady with the white apron who gave me the salmon pâté I bet she would like them, too. When I go back to Bel Air, I will bring her a big bag full of sand crabs. DC finds an old sardine can and gets me a drink of fresh water to finish up.

It's getting dark and chilly, so we go back to our home under the pier. I get in the refrigerator box with DC and curl up on a foam rubber pad next to his beard. It's been a long day. DC strokes my back, and I feel purring-good and soon fall asleep. We both have a very good time together for a couple of weeks living in the box on the beach.

One night, it is pretty cold and damp. DC makes a little fireplace in a big can and stacks up a bunch of little cans for a chimney that goes out the top of our box. He makes a nice little fire with drift-wood. It works very well.

Watching the pretty orange flame, DC says we should always live in a house with a fireplace because fire makes us warm and relaxed. I enjoy looking at the orange flame dancing in our lovely little fireplace. We both fall asleep.

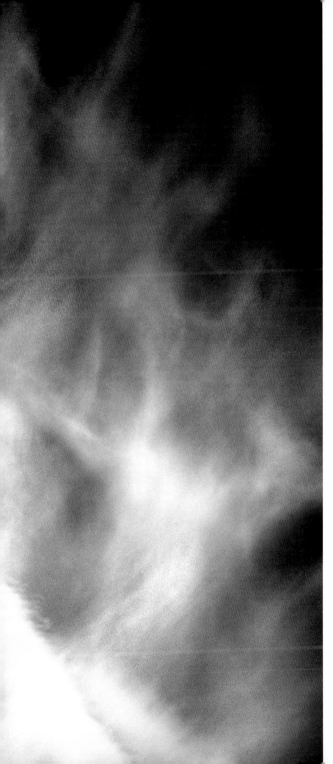

Next thing I know, I am coughing and sneezing because there is smoke inside our box! A lot of gray-and-white smoke fills up our home. I try to wake DC by butting my head on his face. I meow in his ears, bite his arms, scratch his legs. DC does not wake up. I worry about my new friend. He is really asleep. I cough from smoke and push myself out the end of the box, crying. Outside the box, I scream, "MEOW, MEOW, MEOW!" squeezing my voice out from my whole body. "MEOW, MEOW, MEOW!" I see a dark shadow moving on the pier, and I meow even louder. The shadow is a lady who heard me and says, "Kitty, kitty, kitty." I meow back to her. "MEOW, HELP, MEOW!"

"Kitty, where are you? Kitty cat?" She comes down from the pier and finds smoke coming out of the box. She yells, "Oh, my good-ness!" She picks me up, runs to a telephone booth on the pier, and calls the fire department.

Within a few minutes, fire engines with flashing red lights and loud sirens arrive. I'm so scared—I've never been that scared in my whole life. I dig my nails into the lady's arm. She screams with a high pitched voice, "Kitty cat, take it easy, take it easy."

109

The firemen rip open the smoking box and drag DC out. I jump out of the lady's arms and run to him lying on the sand, but one of the firemen stops me. The other one leans over and says, "I don't believe it! It's DC! Hey, DC, what are you doing in here? Wake up." DC moves slowly in response to the fireman's voice. His face is black from the smoke. He is very sick. He opens his eyes halfway, coughs a couple of times, and says, "Where is my pussy cat?" I push between the firemen's legs, jump up on DC's tanned chest, and give him a big snuggle and a smile. He hugs me and gives me kisses.

Suddenly, DC's face is shaking and blurry. I try to focus on it, but all I see is the inside of the box. DC is calling my name. The box shakes hard, opens up, and I see Papa! . . .

"Birthday! What are you doing in the box! Wake up!" And Papa picked me up in his arms. Wow, what a dream! I snuggled into Papa's warm arms.

Mouse Rescue

It was a chilly autumn night. I was about to get into the warm bed where Mama and Papa sleep, but I heard a noise from our kitchen. I walked around the counter in the dark and peeked out at the kitchen floor. There was nobody, but I knew that that was a mouse making those crunching, squeaky noises in the cabinet. I could smell him. I sat in front of the cabinet door and patiently waited. Mama came to the kitchen for a glass of water, and when she opened the refrigerator, the mouse jumped out from under the cabinet. Like a speedball, he ran from the kitchen to the living room and disappeared under a bookshelf. He was tiny, but he moved so fast. I almost caught him, but Mama got in my way. The mouse ran right over Mama's bare foot. Surprised, she let out a scream, and woke Papa up. She almost gave him a heart attack. Boy, she was loud. Disturbed from his deep sleep, Papa turned the lights on.

"What happened?" he asked, frowning. His hair was stuck almost straight up in the air.

"A mouse ran out from under the cabinet and ran across my foot!" Mama replied.

Another disturbing noise interrupted their conversation. Loud sirens and the red and yellow flashing lights of fire engines cut through the dark cold street outside. Papa looked at Mama and asked in low voice, "Did you call 911? Maybe they just heard your scream."

We looked from our window and saw fire engines, ambulances, and police cars quickly moving down the street. A white dog with black spots sitting on one of the fire engines caught my eye. Papa told me that was a dog who rescued people in fires. Wow, what a brave exciting job he had! First time I ever felt respect for dogs. When they all moved away down the street, silence fell in the room. Papa and Mama went back to their bedroom, and Papa turned the lights off. The house fell back to its autumn-night tranquillity.

Lying in my favorite cookie basket on our kitchen counter, I kept thinking about the firedog. "How does he go in the fire? What is he wearing? Isn't he scared of fire? What kind of training does he go through?" Curious me. I wondered so much that I started to imagine myself as a fire cat. I could do his job as long as I didn't get wet! I visualized being among those spotted dogs in the fire department. Suddenly, loud sirens filled the fire station. The firemen, dogs, and I quickly jumped into our uniforms, and I put on two pairs of booties and a helmet. My helmet had a kitty mark on it. Within seconds, we were on the red fire engine moving like a storm, with my nose in the wind, heading toward the house on fire. I had to be the first lady firecat in the world! We arrived at a house with red flames coming out the windows. We jumped out of the engine, and everybody moved very fast and efficiently to do their assigned jobs, just like we had trained every day. I could feel the hot air through the fire-proof suit. I followed my brother firemen and doggies. We all went into the burning house.

EXTRA!

MOUSE RESCUED FROM RAGING FIRE

STORY PAGE 2

TAILY NEWS

Friday, October 4, 2001

MAYOR SALUTES THE BRAVE CAT

HERO CAT!

New York, Oct. 4—Birthday, the first feline firefighter, led the rescue effort in a house fire early this morning. The brave cat successfully brought out a shaky mouse from the blazing house.

BP Photo

Mikky, the mouse, still shaking after being rescued from the blaze, expressed his gratitude to New York's first firecat. He invited her to lunch. When asked if she felt like a hero, Birthday just licked her paws and fell back to sleep.

The fire was a big one and everything was really hot and scary. Everybody was running. I heard people screaming and shouting. I heard a familiar squeaky sound and spotted a mouse crying under an overturned table. The poor mouse was so scared. I ran over and grabbed him by the back of his neck in my mouth and took him outside to an ambulance. The mouse was shaking. He had a sip of water, then said, "Thank you, thank you, Birthday! Thank you for helping me. Thank you for rescuing me. Oh, you saved my life!"

. . . Saved a mouse's life? I opened my eyes and realized I had been dreaming. Still excited and feeling the heat of the fire, I got out of the basket, stretched my back, yawned, then jumped to the floor where my food and water were. Surprise! The little mouse was nibbling my fish cakes. I quietly got close to him and watched him eating. He looked just like the mouse in the fire. He seemed very hungry and didn't notice me at all. When the mouse looked up, his eyes opened so wide, I thought I could see his brain through them. He froze. I said cheerfully, "Hi, I'm Birthday! Are you Mikky?"

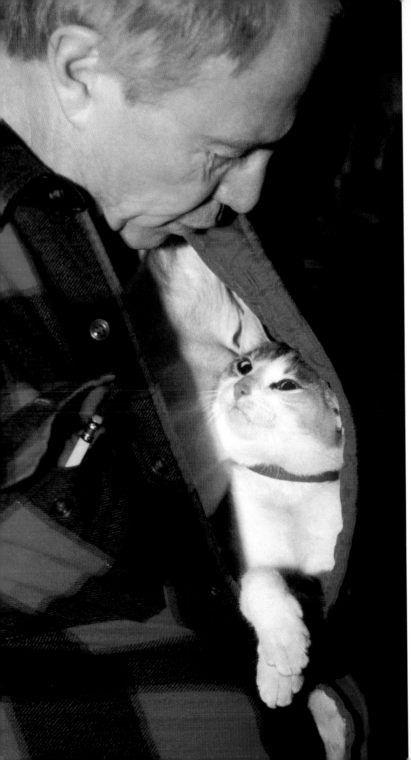

"Are you crazy?" He took off running. I chased him, but he disappeared under the bookshelf again.

In the morning, I told Papa what happened last night. He listened with a smile, then came up with the silly idea of playing with the mouse. He cut a little piece of cheese, tied it to a long string, and put it on my dinner plate. The string was threaded through a hook screwed to the top of the door frame, so it was just like a pulley. Papa pulled on the string, and the cheese went up in the air.

Night came, and so did the mouse. When I heard the crunching, squeaky noise, I woke Papa by pushing my nose against his cheek. He got up quietly, and we sneaked out of the bedroom. We decided not to wake Mama because we didn't want her to scream again. We went to the kitchen quietly. We didn't turn the kitchen lights on, but we could see by the hall light. The little mouse was eating the cheese tied to the string. His cheeks were stuffed. Papa pulled, and the mouse lifted up, his legs running very fast in the air. After a couple of swings, Papa let him down. He took off running with the cheese, and Papa pulled him up in the air again. Papa repeated this many times, but the mouse would not let go of the cheese. Finally, Papa stopped and let him free. The mouse crawled zigzagging until he collapsed on the floor. Papa and I came up and looked at him. He sure was dizzy drunk.

"What should we do?" I asked.

Papa said, "Give him a drink of water."

I picked the mouse up, took him to my bowl, and splashed water on his face. He opened his eyes and drank a lot. He turned around and said to me, "Thank you, thank you, Birthday! Thank you for helping me. Thank you for rescuing me. Oh, you saved my life!"

"Well," I thought, "there goes my good cat reputation." Then he quickly took off running.

Mama came to kitchen and said, "What are you two doing in the kitchen in the middle of the night? Is there a mouse again?"

"What mouse?" Papa and I looked at each other and cracked up laughing.

I started very young practicing mouse wrestling . . .
I mean, rescue.

Sharing dreams

Two couch spuds

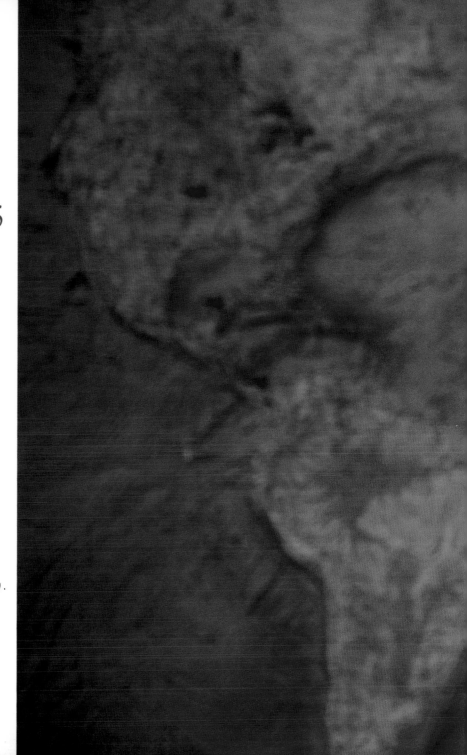

Travel Snaps

Papa says I'm working on
my frequent-liar-miles
program.

Deep breath under blue sky

Wildcat in Canyonlands

Making a new friend is another wonderful reason to travel.

Kitten in the Park

Where am I?

When I was little, I often went to Central Park with Mama and Papa. I enjoyed riding on Papa's head or shoulder and marching around the beautiful park. He would always wear a hat, and I would lay my belly on his head and rest my front paws on the brim. People passing by would always give us big smiles, and I would wave to them with my tail. Sometimes Papa would let me down on the ground, and I could walk free. Well, I did have to wear a leash on my neck like a dog. Walking in the park was exciting—if Papa didn't pull me too often. I told him that when I'm on a leash and walking, I should be in charge of the direction. He agreed, but if I sniffed in one location too long, he couldn't wait and carried me to another place. Sometimes, he didn't want me to climb a tree if it was too tall because he  wouldn't be able to follow me—at least, that's what he said. People found it unusual that a cat was walking on a leash. I like being in the park, but getting there is a pain in the neck. I hate being surrounded by loud scary traffic noises on the streets. Riding the subway is not so bad, but sometimes it is extremely noisy, too. Well, sometimes if you bear pain, the relief you feel when it goes away can give you pleasure. So, when I get to the park, I enjoy soaking the warm sun into my fuzzy fur under the blue sky.

This happened on one of those fun afternoons in early summer. I met a pretty little girl, Luci, in the park. She had beautiful curly blonde hair that was almost transparent, and the golden sunlight filtered through it. I was happy to meet her because she smelled like sunshine. Luci was with her mother, and all of us sat together on the young soft green grass under a big old oak tree. While my parents and her mama were having a good time talking, Luci tossed me a little red rubber ball and said, "Birthday, let's play!"

The little ball bounced on the grass, then stopped between us. I ran to it and kicked it back to her with my front paw. She chased the rolling ball, running and chuckling. Her happy voice soared into the blue sky. The ball rolled back and forth between us many, many times. It was a lot of fun. She threw the ball again; this time it rolled down the hill. She ran after the red ball, and I followed her. It rolled faster and faster, then disappeared in a bush, and we stopped at the bottom of the hill.

Catching her breath, she asked me, "Where did it go?" I was out of breath, too. With my heart beating very fast, I said, "I think it went into this bush."

I stepped in, and she followed me. While I was creeping and sniffing, I heard a cry. I stopped moving and tried to find out where the cry was coming from and who made it. "Did you find the ball?" she asked.

"I heard someone crying."

Luci didn't hear anything, but I was sure I heard a baby crying.

She tucked her fluffy golden curls behind her ears and with her hands, pushed her ears forward. "Like an elephant. I can hear better," she explained with a smile. We focused on the cry. I heard it again. It came from the willow tree by the pond. This time she heard it also, and cried, "It sounds like a kitty!"

We left the bush and found a kitten in a box under the willow. I stood a distance away from the box—it scared me. I knew the cry. I knew what he wanted. He was calling for his mother. Where was his mother? All of the remembered sadness and anger came back to me and I couldn't move. I stood still. I could hear his desperate meows, his little nails scratching on the cardboard box. A long branch of the green willow swayed softly into the box as if the tree was comforting the baby. Luci reached in and lifted the kitten from the box. He was a tiny fuzzy gray creature. His eyes were still closed, and his small ears hung almost from the sides of his head. I couldn't believe how small he was and how loud his cries were.

"Kitty, kitty. Stop crying, little kitty." Luci tried to comfort him, but he continued to cry. She said, "You should be his mother, Birthday."

How silly! I was only a child myself. I didn't know what to say to the crying baby. I started crying, too.

With two cats crying loudly, people started to gather around us. Soon Luci's mother and my parents found us in the center of a crowd. Luci handed the crying kitten to her mom, telling her that we found him in the box. People were all looking at me because I was crying even louder next to the empty box. "Birthday!" Mama picked me up, and I stopped crying. The tiny kitty was still meowing in Luci's mother's hands.

Papa said, "He must be hungry."

Luci asked, "Can Birthday give him some milk?"

Papa replied for me. "No, Birthday is not his mother, and she is still too young to be a mother."

Luci rubbed my head and gave me a sweet kiss.

"What should we do?" Luci's mother asked Papa.

"Well, do you want to take him home?" Papa asked back. She said they had small birds at home and were afraid to have a cat in their house. Papa looked at me and Mama. We all nodded. "Let's take him with us."

We said good-bye to Luci and her mother, then headed back home.

Papa bought special milk for the baby kitten, who cried all the way home. Papa warmed the milk and put it into a bottle for him, just like he did for me when I first came home. It was strange to see someone drinking from my little bottle. I remembered how quickly the warm milk filled up my body and my heart. But the kitten did not drink much. He stopped crying and slept for a while. He must have been tired of crying. I asked Mama if I was that small when I came home. She said I was bigger than him even though she thought I was tiny. My eyes were already open, and they were blue gray. We each took a turn feeding the kitten, but he hardly drank. He cried most of that night. Next day, Papa bought different milk, but the same thing happened. The kitten didn't take any. He just cried. He cried so loud, but we couldn't help. I told him he should drink more milk so his belly would get warm and he could stop crying, but he just cried. I asked him his name, he didn't know.

I wondered what happened to his mother.

On the third day, we were really concerned for the kitten, because he wouldn't drink anything, and he was getting very weak. His meow was not so loud anymore. I told Papa the kitten should see my doctor. Papa called my doctor and made an appointment for the afternoon. As soon as Papa hung up, we heard the kitten burst out crying. I leaned over to him. "Don't be afraid. He is a good doctor."

Then Mama said, "I hear another cat meowing from outside." She opened a window and there was a big gray cat at our front door looking straight up and crying at her. Mama and Papa ran down the steps and opened the front door. The gray cat made one step into the doorway, then sat there very politely, urging us to return her baby. She was the kitten's mother! She explained to us how she got separated from her baby when her owner decided not to keep it. She ran away from home in search of her baby all over the city, almost getting hit by a car. She found the box in the park when she was just about to give up the search. The smell of her baby in the empty box energized her. At same time, she started to worry about whether her baby had a new mother already because she smelled my tears on the box. From there, she frantically traced the smell of her baby and me, and finally found our home. She seemed tired, but her tension was very high. She did not come up our steps, but patiently waited for our permission to take her baby. The kitten was in our living room crying with a high-pitched voice, and we could hear him all the way downstairs. If the mother cat wanted to run up the steps and grab the baby, she easily could have, but she was extremely polite. Instead, I ran up, grabbed the kitty in my mouth, then slowly walked down the steps to the front door. When the mother cat saw her

baby, she meowed intensely, and as soon as I put the baby down in front of her, she picked him up and ran away. I saw a spark of joy from both of them.

Mama and Papa couldn't comprehend the intensity of the mother cat. We were in shock and stood at the door for a moment, until Papa went outside to see where they went. But they had left without a trace. We talked about them all day. It was amazing. By dinnertime, we were happy the kitty and his mother were together, and we toasted them, wishing them a happy life. "Meow!"

Kiss to Mama!

Kiss to Papa!

Vermont Fairy Tale

I have met fairies.

This is not something I talk about often, because you may think I am nuts. I'm not a nut. I may be a banana sometimes, but never a nut. The fairies I saw live in Vermont, in a real house made with sweet sugar. If you ever have a chance to go there, you will know what I mean. The house belongs to our dear friends Auntie Sonja and Uncle Angelo. You can feel their love inside and outside and all through the woods.

To tell you about the fairies I met, I must explain a little more about this special house. The old Vermont farmhouse sits on a hill of green grass and wild flowers, surrounded by many, many old trees. As you drive up through a tunnel of old maple trees, a cute red house appears, welcoming you with a warm, loving smile. You sense the quiet hum of the trees and flowers around the house.

I remember the very first time I stepped on the grass dotted with red and yellow autumn leaves. An apple fell on the ground in front of me. I grabbed the stem in my mouth and brought the small red apple to Auntie Sonja. She smiled. Mama and Papa picked more apples from the tree and peeled them while we all sat on the grass. They became sweet-tart applesauce. I kept the stem. The house paints itself on the surface of the shimmering pond behind it. Mama told me she had gone swimming in the pond

with Auntie Sonja that summer. I bet she swam with frogs, too. Not for me. I don't like to swim, but I sort of like frogs. I had a taste of the springwater. It made me feel good, so I had more. The colors of the leaves were particularly glorious that year; there was nothing like it. There were so many colors; red, orange, yellow, and green, sprinkling from the blue sky like confetti all over Vermont. We enjoyed soaking ourselves in the celebration of colors all day long. It was unbelievably beautiful.

Before the sun went down, we settled in and lit the inside of the house with two gaslights in the kitchen and living room. This house lives without electricity. The gaslights are as bright as any electric lamps, and they have a warm, welcoming glow, helping people to see, cook, and read at night. To go into other rooms, we had to carry candles or flashlights. When Papa walked into the bathroom, he reached for a wall switch to turn on. He realized there was nothing to flip and laughed. Mama did the same thing. We learned that the flame of a candle can light up a whole room. It's not a bright light, but it's enough to see what's around you. Two or three candle lights illuminate a whole room like a center stage. Papa's and Mama's shadows danced with the flame. I like candle lights. Mama and Auntie Sonja were together in the kitchen laughing and cooking dinner. They cooked trout and chanterelle mushrooms, which we had picked in the woods that day. Auntie Sonja was very good at picking up mushrooms. Papa and Uncle Angelo put firewood in the potbellied stove. It gets a little chilly at night in Vermont. Everyone had drinks and laughed at tons of jokes. They all had a great time. So I was free to be myself.

There were so many sweet smells I wanted to sniff in this house. Listening to their laughter, I walked up and down the stairs to sniff. I felt tickling-happy myself.

After our bellies were filled with delicious trout and special mushrooms, the quiet night fell upon us. Everyone sat silently in front of the warm pot-bellied stove, making themselves comfortable. I got on the dinner table, where a red candle was still lit. I stared at the flame for a long time. I was mesmerized by its beauty.

Fire always fascinates me.

Suddenly, I heard a giggle. I put my ears up and turned around, but there was no one in the room. I kept my eyes on the orange light. I didn't blink. I heard the same giggle again. It seemed to be coming from the candle light. I stared through the orange flame. As I focused hard on the flame, I saw something dancing in the candle light, chuckling and beckoning to me. There were small creatures with beautiful multicolored wings and smiling faces jumping and hopping in the flame. They said, "Come on, Birthday. Play with us!" and they chuckled.

They were so joyful! My heart beat with delight from this wonderful discovery. I wanted to dance with them. I reached in the flame to touch their hands, but they gave me HOT kisses! They were burning hot, so I licked my paw. The kisses tasted bittersweet with a hint of mint. So I reached in to touch them again. Then I heard Mama and Papa laughing. Papa said, "Birthday, what are you doing with the candle?"

Auntie Sonja smiled and said, "Oh, Birthday just met the fire fairies!"

I'll see you again.

Happy Birthday, every day!

Book ends here. Meow!